Whale of a Tale

Written by Peter Millett
Illustrated by John Bennett

Grandpa pulled his boat out of the shed and handed Thomas and Justine their life jackets. He was going to take them out onto the bay for a fishing trip.

"Are you ready for an exciting adventure?" he asked. "I can already feel the fish starting to bite. Today's the day I'm going to catch the big one."

Grandma laughed loudly.

"That's the same story you tell me every day you go out fishing. But, somehow, the big one always manages to get away.

"You kids, don't listen to a word of your grandfather's ocean tales. They're all made up."

Grandpa pushed his boat into the water.

"See you at lunchtime, " he shouted to Grandma.

Out in the bay, Justine watched her grandfather tease the fish with his home-made bait.

"Grandpa, is it true that you once caught a giant squid?"

"Oh, yes... yes I did. It was a terrible monster. Its eyes were bigger than bicycle wheels."

"Did you get a photo of it?"

"Um, no I didn't. It was too quick for me. It jumped out of the net before I could find my camera. The big ones always seem to get away. But, I'm glad it did though. That beast could have swallowed me whole and still had room left for breakfast, lunch and dinner."

"Really?" said Justine, laughing.

Boom! Suddenly, the small boat rocked back and forth.

"What's happening?" yelled Justine.

"SHARK!" cried Thomas.

Justine screamed.

Grandpa looked over the side of the boat. **Whoosh!** A huge spurt of water shot skywards.

"It's a whale!" he cried, pointing at a black bump rising up out of the sea.

"A whale... in the bay?" shouted Thomas.

Justine grabbed her grandfather's arm.

"Grandpa, are we safe in here?"

Grandpa hugged her.

"Don't worry, we're really safe. But that big fella is going to be in a whole lot of trouble if he keeps on swimming towards the beach."

Grandpa turned his boat around to try and head off the whale. He looked worried.

"If the whale strands itself on the beach, then all of the other whales will come in and strand themselves as well."

Thomas waved his arms wildly at the whale, trying to steer it away from the beach. But it was no use. The whale kept on swimming through the shallow waters.

Suddenly, it hit a sand bar and skidded up onto the beach.

"Oh... this is not good, " cried Grandpa.

Grandpa sped his boat up onto the sand. He jumped out and ran to his house.

He yelled for Grandma, banging on the window. But there was no reply. "Your grandmother picked a fine time to be out shopping," he said.

"What are we going to do?" cried Justine. "We've got to stop the other whales from coming in."

Grandpa looked at the whale flapping its tail helplessly on the sand. "Okay, I've got a plan. You kids grab as many wet towels as you can find and cover up the whale. I'll start the rescue mission."

Thomas and Justine pulled all of the towels off the clothesline and carried them down to the water. They soaked them and placed them over the whale to try and keep it cool and wet.

Grandpa jumped on his old beach tractor.

Vroom-vroom!

He fired up its noisy engine.

"What are you doing?" cried Thomas.

"When I was in the navy, we had to rescue a submarine that got stuck on a beach. I think this big fella looks a bit like a submarine, so maybe the same trick will work for him, too."

Grandpa carefully tied some rope around the whale's tail and hooked it up to the back of his tractor.

Vroom! He gunned the tractor's engine and slowly began dragging the whale into the sea.

"Easy does it," he cried, looking over his shoulder.

When the water was waist deep, he swung the tractor hard to his left, turning the whale around in a circle. Soon, the whale was facing back out to sea. Grandpa released the rope around its tail and gave it a huge push.

"Swim, big fella, swim!"

Splosh!

The whale slapped its tail down and began swimming.

"Yahoo," yelled Justine, jumping up and down in the sand.

Grandpa cheered as he watched the whale swim across the bay and head out towards the open ocean.

Just then, Grandma arrived home. "You're all back very early from your fishing trip," she said.

She glared at Grandpa.

"Now, let me guess — the big one got away again, did it?"

Grandpa laughed and shrugged his shoulders.

Thomas grabbed his grandmother's arm and tugged at it excitedly. "It sure did, Grandma — and now it's safely back out at sea!"

Whale of a Tale is a Narrative.

A narrative has an introduction. It tells . . .

* **who** the story is about (the characters)

* **where** the story happened

* **when** the story happened.

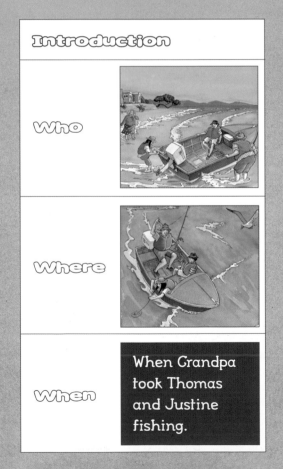

A narrative has a **problem** and a **solution**.

Problem

Solution

▬▬▬ Guide Notes

Title: Whale of a Tale
Stage: Fluency

Text Form: Narrative
Approach: Guided Reading
Processes: Thinking Critically, Exploring Language, Processing Information
Written and Visual Focus: Illustrative Text

THINKING CRITICALLY
(sample questions)
- What do you think this story could be about? Look at the title and discuss.
- Look at the cover. Why do you think the whale is jumping out of the water?
- Look at pages 2 and 3. Why do you think "the big one always manages to get away"?
- Look at pages 4 and 5. Do you think Grandpa really once caught a giant squid? Why do you think that?
- Look at pages 6 and 7. Why do you think the whale is going to be in trouble if it keeps on swimming towards the beach?
- Look at pages 8 and 9. Why do you think the other whales might come in and strand themselves as well?
- Look at pages 10 and 11. What does "rescue mission" mean? What do you think Grandpa and the children can do to help the whale?
- Look at pages 12 and 13. What do you think the "same trick" might be?

EXPLORING LANGUAGE

Terminology
Spread, author and illustrator credits, imprint information, ISBN number

Vocabulary
Clarify: life jackets, bait, squid, strand, sand bar, rescue mission, tractor, engine, navy, submarine
Adjectives: *exciting* adventure, *home-made* bait, *terrible* monster
Pronouns: you, it, he, his, I, me, her
Adverbs: laughed *loudly*, waved his arms *wildly*, flapping its tail *helplessly*, tugged at it *excitedly*
Focus the students' attention on **homonyms**, **antonyms** and **synonyms** if appropriate.